W9-CIQ-898

AN ALPHABET OF ROTTEN KIDS!

AN ALPHABET OF
Rotten Kids!

By **DAVID ELLIOTT**
Art by **OSCAR de MEJO**

PHILOMEL BOOKS New York

A | Agatha | B | Bartholomew | C | Chelsea | D | Dominic | E | Ernestine | F
Zazu
Z | Yolanda | Ferdinand
Y | Xerxes | G | Georgina
X | Wilhelmina | H | Horatio
W | Vincent | I | Imogene
V | Ursula | J | Jacob
U | Tip, Tolly | K | Katrina
T | Sabrina | L | Lionel
S | | M | Margarite
| ...intana | Q | Peter, Paul, Pip, Perry | P | Oona | O | Nasty Ned | N

Text copyright © 1991 by David Elliott
Illustrations copyright © 1991 by Oscar de Mejo
Published by Philomel Books, a division of
The Putnam & Grosset Book Group, 200 Madison
Avenue, New York, NY 10016. Published simultaneously
in Canada. All rights reserved.
Typography by Kathleen Westray
Printed in Hong Kong by South China Printing Co. (1988) Ltd.

First impression.

Library of Congress Cataloging-in-Publication Data
Elliott, David, 1947—
An alphabet of rotten kids!/by David Elliott.
p.   cm.
Summary: Twenty-six poems about children who misbehave,
arranged in alphabetical order from Agatha to Zazu.
ISBN 0-399-22260-X
1. Behavior disorders in children—Juvenile poetry. 2. Children's
poetry, American. 3. Alphabet rhymes. [1. Behavior—Poetry.
2. Alphabet. 3. American poetry. 4. II no ills. FA05 04-27-90.]
PS3555.L5674A47 1991 811'.54—dc20 [E] 90-35588 CIP AC

To my sisters, Sharon and Glory
—DE

To all the good children in the world
—OdM

A

Agatha,
bad as they come,
not nearly though as bad as some,
took a wad of chewing gum
and stuck her elbow to her thumb.

Oh, Agatha!

B

Bartholomew,
who will do for *B*,
poured ink into his teacher's tea.
Her lips turned blue as the Coral Sea.
So sad for one just twenty-three.

Oh, Bartholomew!

C

Chelsea,
a very wicked child,
pretended to be weak and mild.
She drove the babysitter wild!
But when asked why, she only smiled.

Oh, Chelsea!

D
Dominic,
yes, Dominic,
his hair combed back all nice and slick,
did something dreadful with a brick.
But blamed it on his brother, Rick.

Oh, Dominic!

E Perhaps you've heard
of Ernestine,
who painted her French poodle green,
something like a lima bean.
Poor thing! It never did get clean.

Oh, Ernestine!

Ferdinand,
that little squirt,
filled the living room with dirt.
When spanked, he told his cousin, Bert,
"So what! It didn't even hurt!"

Oh, Ferdinand!

G Georgina,
with such curly hair,
cut a hole in her underwear.
She said she didn't really care
because no one ever saw her there.

Oh, Georgina!

H
Horatio,
bad as you please,
would stuff his mouth with frozen peas.
His teeth would click, his tongue would freeze
and then, mouth full of peas, he'd sneeze!

Yech, Horatio!

I Imogene,
who is our *I*,
told all the neighbors she could fly.
But every last one wondered why
they never saw her in the sky.

Oh, Imogene!

J Jacob,
also known as Jake,
wondered how long it would take
his mom to find the rubber snake
he hid inside her chocolate cake.

Oh, Jacob!

K Katrina K,
cute as a bug,
jumped into a hole she'd dug
and gave herself a little hug
for cutting up the upstairs rug.

Oh, Katrina!

L Lionel,
that little rat,
sat upon his father's hat.
He tried to say it was the cat,
who thought he was a perfect brat.

Oh, Lionel!

M

**For *M*
we will choose Margarite,
who everybody thought so sweet
until she grabbed the Sunday meat
and shoved it down the parakeet.**

Oh, Margarite!

N

N will stand
for Nasty Ned,
who had such things inside his head,
his aunts and uncles turned bright red
when they heard the things he said.

Shhhhh, Ned!

O

Oona,
with so many *O*'s,
stuffed a bean inside her nose.
She said, "I surely hope it grows,"
then went outside to find the hose.

Oooooo, Oona!

P Peter, Paul,
Pip, and Perry
decided it would be quite merry
to play a trick on Jill and Jerry.
What they did was scary! Very!

Oh, Peter! Oh, Paul! Oh, Pip! Oh, Perry!

Q

Quintana,
which begins with *Q*,
does what all the bad kids do.
She has a tube of Power glue.
I'd look out if I were you!

Oh, Quintana!

R
Raoul, Raoul,
Raoul, Raoul.
His mother thought he was a jewel.
But kids called him Raoul the Ghoul
because he bit them, as a rule.

Ouch, Raoul!

S Sabrina,
who will stand for *S*,
put on her brand new party dress
and took a shower. What a mess!
She didn't like that dress, I guess.

Oh, Sabrina!

Tip and Tolly,
terrible twins,
where one leaves off, the other begins,
bought a box of safety pins.
Now Tip cries while Tolly grins.

Poor Tip! No, Tolly!

U

Ursula,
who carried a purse,
taught all the other kids to curse.
She said she learned it from a nurse.
Somehow, that seemed to make it worse.

#*& + ! Ursula!

V

Vincent
who was no saint,
drank several tubs of finger paint.
After which he'd one complaint:
"I thought it would be good. It ain't!"

Oh, Vincent!

W

Wilhelmina,
sometimes called Willie,
made a pot of red hot chili,
then served it up to Mike and Millie,
who in the end went willy-nilly!

Oh, Willie!

XYZ

Xerxes,
Yolanda, and Zazu
do things I know I wouldn't do!
(Well, I might do one or two
if I thought you'd do them, too.)

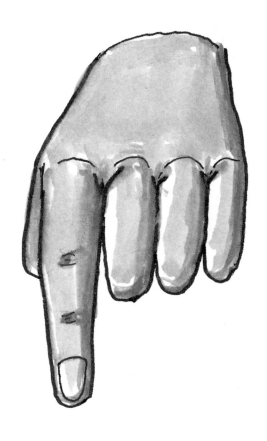

Would you?